Further Praise for *The*

"With a dose of self-awareness that is by turns playful, thought-provoking, and heartbreaking, the poems in [*The Absurd Man*] offer up a collective narrative to complement their stand-alone lyricism. . . . A standout collection with many a standout poem."
—Grant Schatzman, *World Literature Today*

"The poems in *The Absurd Man* are philosophical, imaginative, and self-aware, by turns humorous and deeply serious. . . . [E]verything Jackson excels at is on display. The diction, syntax, and musical elements, including end rhymes and alliteration, result in a flow of rich, textured language, as well-made as it feels effortless."
—Gardner McFall, *Literary Matters*

"Shimmering. . . . Jackson's eye is laser-sharp and wry. . . . Throughout the book, [his] weaving of mythology and literary references serve as context for confrontations with personal ghosts. . . . In this accomplished work, readers will find that absurdity is only a stop along the road to larger meaning."
—*Publishers Weekly*, starred review

"In a heady, meditative work eschewing facile topicality and equally facile navel gazing, Jackson ambitiously posits himself as the absurd hero of Albert Camus's *The Myth of Sisyphus* to grapple with contemporary malaise."
—*Library Journal*, "Best Books of 2020"

"Poems in Major Jackson's *The Absurd Man* are fashioned from masks and personae, impersonations and thrown voices. How ironic then that this fifth and most daring book yet sings deeply, solemn and vulnerable, a blues for our times. One of the root meanings of the word *absurd* is 'out of tune.' To be out of tune with these years of American absurdity,

Jackson's adroit lyrics resonate through a kind of fission, the collision of selves and personal histories yielding a most genuine ore. These poems face the music of their own making."

—Gregory Pardlo, Pulitzer Prize–winning author of *Digest*

"At the end of his richly introspective and engagingly vulnerable collection, *The Absurd Man*, Major Jackson, referring to his double self, also a character in the collection, observes wryly, 'Tragically, he believes he can mend his wounds with his poetry.' And in this everything hopeful, elegant, daring, and unsettlingly absurd about *The Absurd Man* is spoken. Jackson embraces the existential absurdity of this 'tragedy' and yet, in doing so, he gives us poems that dare to challenge hopelessness with language."

—Kwame Dawes, author of *City of Bones*

THE ABSURD MAN

THE ABSURD MAN

POEMS

Major Jackson

W. W. NORTON & COMPANY
Independent Publishers Since 1923

For information about permission to reproduce selections from this book, write to
Permissions, W. W. Norton & Company, Inc., 500 Fifth Avenue, New York, NY 10110

For information about special discounts for bulk purchases, please contact
W. W. Norton Special Sales at specialsales@wwnorton.com or 800-233-4830

Manufacturing by LSC Communications, Harrisonburg
Book design by Chris Welch
Production manager: Anna Oler

Library of Congress Cataloging-in-Publication Data

Names: Jackson, Major, 1968–author.
Title: The absurd man : poems / Major Jackson.
Description: First edition. | New York : W. W. Norton & Company, [2020]
Identifiers: LCCN 2019045399 | ISBN 9781324004554 (hardcover) |
ISBN 9781324004561 (epub)
Subjects: LCGFT: Poetry.
Classification: LCC PS3610.A354 A63 2020 | DDC 811/.6—dc23
LC record available at https://lccn.loc.gov/2019045399

ISBN 978-0-393-86741-1 pbk.

W. W. Norton & Company, Inc., 500 Fifth Avenue, New York, N.Y. 10110
www.wwnorton.com
W. W. Norton & Company Ltd., 15 Carlisle Street, London W1D 3BS

1 2 3 4 5 6 7 8 9 0

for Jill Bialosky

CONTENTS

A FRENZY OF DESIGNS FROM THE AGE OF ENLIGHTENMENT

A FRENZY OF DESIGNS FROM THE AGE OF ENLIGHTENMENT

What, in fact, is the absurd man? He who, without negating it, does nothing for the eternal. Not that nostalgia is foreign to him. But he prefers his courage and his reasoning.

—*The Myth of Sisyphus*, Albert Camus

    hand in hand remove our dark suits, but
the other Major prefers to undress in glass
revolving doors; he is a fan of prohibition
cocktails whose potions afford him time-travels
of the landed gentry. I let Major sport
his dangers which magnify his ambitions
so he can write his grandiloquent poems,
and thus, ours is a compromised relationship:
I, more cautious than a slug, and he,
the sampler of pythons.
    Major is a fan of Peruvian folk songs,
wood-paneled libraries, rare colognes, and old
issues of *Esquire*. I, on the other hand, prefer
American football, treasury bills, and vintage
sports cars. Only once did I try to escape
his clutches, this other Major.
    For years I survived his rank
songs which make the Spanish cantors weep.
His fingers carry the bitter taste of coffee,
which, occasionally, I sniff, for they are
the color of ancient bark. Forgive his pretenses, he
who wrote that last sentence. It is probably

true he wrote most of this, but I am unsure
for I live just behind him, a single keystroke
shy of his many thoughts. Beware
his black rituals.

    The other Major flies in his daydreams
which means he's collecting a paradise
of mirrors where I sit studying the prose
of Toomer, Morrison, and Faulkner. Latinate
though he is, master of the outside, he digs
the gangster lean and is more thankful
than a sunroof top. His broken strings, like
his stubble, issue forth a wintry path
at night for white walls. See what I mean?

    Major never won attendance awards,
and for sure long ago he left behind
cigarettes and the guarded strips of lotto
tickets but cherishes still the big hit. Admit
his charms and you've a friend for life.
He will send you sunflowers (true),
even from his coffin (not true), and although
he never learned to play the violin or the mouth
harp, a radio plays like an all-night laundromat
behind his eyes, and thus, he lives year-round
in the boot camp of self-redemption;
for this the other Major needs lots
of sky. You are that sky.

YOU, READER

So often I dream of the secrets of satellites,
and so often I want the moose to step
from the shadows and reveal his transgressions,
and so often I come to her body
as though she were Lookout Mountain,
but give me a farmers' market to park my martyred masks
and I will name all the dirt roads that dead-end
at the cubist sculpture called *My Infinity*,
for I no longer light bonfires in the city of adulterers
and no longer smudge the cheeks of debutantes
hurriedly floating across the high fruit of night,
and yes, I know there is only one notable death in any small town
and that is the pig farmer, but listen, at all times
the proud rivers mourn my absence, especially
when, like a full moon, you, reader, hidden behind a spray
of night-blooming, drift in and out of scattered clouds
above lighthouses producing their artificial calm,
just to sweep a chalk of light over distant waters.

THE FLÂNEUR TENDS A WELL-LIKED
SUMMER COCKTAIL

curbside on an Arp-like table. He's alone
of course, in the arts district as it were, legs folded,
swaying a foot so that his body seems to summon
some deep immensity from all that surrounds:
dusk shadows inching near a late-thirtyish couple debating
the post-galactic abyss of sex with strangers,
tourists ambling by only to disappear into the street's gloomy mouth,
a young Italian woman bending to retrieve
a dropped MetroCard, its black magnetic strip facing up,
a lone speckled brown pigeon breaking from a flock of rock
doves, then landing near a crushed fast-food wrapper
newly tossed by a bike messenger, the man chortling
after a sip of flaxen-colored beer, remembering
that, in the Gospel of John the body and glory converge
linked to incarnation and so, perhaps, we manifest each other,
a tiny shower of sparks erupting from the knife sharpener's
truck who daily leans a blade into stone, a cloudscape reflected
in the rear windshield of a halted taxi where inside
a trans woman applies auburn lipstick, the warlike
insignia on the lapel jacket of a white-gloved
doorman who opening a glass door gets a whiff

of a dowager's thick perfume and recalls baling timothy
hay as a boy in Albania, the woman distractedly watching
a mother discuss Robert Colescott's lurid appropriations
of modernist art over niçoise salad, suddenly frees her left breast
from its cup where awaits the blossoming mouth of an infant
wildly reaching for a galaxy of milk, the sharp coughs
of a student carrying a yoga mat, the day's last light edging
high-rises on the West Side so that they seem rimmed
by fire just when the man says, And yet, immense the wages
we pay boarding the great carousel of flesh.

GOING INTO BATTLE

The birthmark on the lower right
of my wife's back is a letter of resurrection.
Each night I kiss it before I turn out the lights
so that it blesses my sleep.

A stamp of all her sorrows,
I regard it with the utmost importance,
for it sets her apart from all other creatures.
Sometimes I put my face to its amoeba-like shape
to see if I can hear the long wail of her creation.

Periodically it guides me across the waters
of my absent desire like a beacon,
only brown and lightly spotted.

One before saw it as a sign of war and created a sentinel
around his body, and he who beheld it next heard
the rattling of dice in a gambler's hand.

I am the only one who makes peace before facing
the large screen of dreams, knowing a wind-cursed
city lies behind my eyelids.

THE FLAG OF IMAGINATION FURLED

In the middle of March, the sky over Siena
faded like a roar but not the tenants
of cemeteries, for I had not learned to wrestle
the hours nor solved the great riddles
in the narrow districts of my glass-encased cities.
What overcame me, all that running my forefinger
down the wintry pages of my masters
and my adversaries, touching
their sentences like sculptured palaces,
touring their villages of ink? I'm sure
Nina Simone was there and helped to deepen
the pouches beneath my eyes even in gleeful Madrid,
even as I preached to a cloistered community, close-knit
as a garlic clove or spray-painted morning fog, avoiding
the lash of geraniums lest it launch me into a spell
of lyric wonder. Severe sadness? A cocoon of oppression?
Nothing accounted for my frozen laughter in the proud
cantinas, my meticulous lack of holy clamor as I scribbled
toward some infinitude. How often I've wanted to
cruise my mirrors or pose questions to my footsteps,
of course without the crisis of caves or politicians

eating hungrily from their dark bowls of pocket watches.
There is, within me, an invincible summer,
a seasonal wind, and my name is on it.

NOVEMBER IN XICHANG

There are cities one won't see again.

—JOSEPH BRODSKY

1.

Only a bearded smile shows below a conical hat
turning men to rice farmers or Wang Lung pulling
a rickshaw except I'm on a bamboo raft
guided by a soundless Charon whose wooden pole
dips into the Qionghai, spiking dead lotus
flowers. Were this pottery from one of those dynasties,
Ming or Han, there'd be a pagoda, an arching bridge, and us
on a blue and white plate in silk robes, practicing pieties,
forever gazing, as on Keats's urn, though ravished in dry reeds.

2.

The mountains shy at my early arrival, clouds like tangled
lingerie still skirting their range. Up to ankles
in sedge grass, a discouraged heron gawkily aims
for a higher floor then gives a raspy cluck, declaiming
in birdspeak, "There goes the neighborhood."

I want to embrace this scene for all its good,
yet how, with you hotel-bound, coughing, bedridden?
The lake's quiet surface enters my spine; the hidden
marvels suddenly made visible like a torch from a flame.

3.

That stilled fisherman inked to a shadow inhabits
a hanging scroll I've made in my mind,
his back to net and rods, a panel perhaps in classic
script, ideograms spelling out the swiftness of time,
vertically, of course, as he tries to stare
past weed muck into a future obscured,
as we are, by an understory of shriveled lily pads,
by reflection of an osier's spilling hair. You've had
it with crumpled tissues piling up like drafts.

4.

You've had it with traditional healing teas,
cigarette smoke dragoning through walls.
You've had it with squatting stalls
but not the hospitality of the Yi,
their rotating trays, lamb's tongue, hot pots,

beef and bladder, old-style songs, folk
dances, the falsetto notes of the men, the pitch
of cool in poncho-frayed white cloaks,
the ways to say "beautiful" in everyone's thoughts.

5.

Last night I proclaimed art as a container
for the self on a panel echoing Whitman
then worried I too loudly banged the drum.
Our Chinese friends, tolerant of my campaign
for a spirit radiant as the gold on their flag, clapped
like flickering stars at the end of my speech.
Today, I calm my fears: spy movies, wiretaps,
casual surveillance, the feeling of being watched,
the terrors that enter the room while we sleep.

6.

We steel ourselves despite the filigreed
air, sunlight rendering more real the horror,
our cameras pointing to blood gushing like water
in a rural courtyard. Circled around a table,
our senses empty as fast as lacquer goblets fill.

Nearby, behind a cage, preparing himself for the playbill
featuring himself, a pig practices his squealing
last act. New Year's Day, "Ku Shi" in Yi,
six invisible days but first a slaughter.

7.

In theater seats, in the outdoor air of night,
our eyes focus on a water curtain, a projected eagle
flapping slow-motion: choreographed flames ignite
Heaven's Fire: The Totem of Life but I find its sequel
later in our room without the flashing lights or fountains
shooting their aquatic cannons. What synchronizes
beneath sheets like a lunar eclipse, a *Fragrance
of Years*, a wish, when one partner dies
and the other no longer hears a peacock's screeching cry.

8.

Our wish for faith leads us to Quan Yin visible
on the horizon above village houses. Off tour
we pass through narrow streets seeking her temple,
then plant sticks of incense like flags, give our
three prostrations and pray for compassion.

An old woman whose creases long ago marbled
her face, speaks gentle as coiled smoke. I imagine
her blessing us, strangers in her land who marvel
at the slightest kindness, evidence of a human circle.

9.

Though air around us feels like a shrine,
we become creatures of the treaties
of gestures, seeking nonverbal speech that rhymes
with our curiosities, faces that unlock cities
so the massive doors of indifference swing open
and what's revealed, a bright garden that leads toward
some miracle of air. In the Yi Slavery Museum, a Bimo's
screeching dispossession of cries and words
reminds me: we have only each other in the end.

MY CHILDREN'S INHERITANCE

A fancy for high green hills by a sea, baggy spaces
    in the day, a knack for gunpowder thinking,
a library humming like a swarm of gnats;

the intrigue of a woman with a pitch-perfect mind,
    blinking eyes whose silence is ancient and naked,
a grave, which is not a grave, but a ruin to visit in middle age;

a chifforobe of half-empty cologne bottles in various colors
    and dried flowers more dignified in death, both
evidence that I once cherished bouquets and timelessness;

bullet casings, a bowl of seashells, fine pens, one
    the *Aurora Diamante* with its two-toned rhodium-plating
that glitters when my right hand rages toward heaven;

a love of big plates of pasta, Argentinian folk music,
    African rainforests and the speeches of Lincoln that
mist the pages of my books more than my doorways;

a habit of dancing when the needle drops its existential beats,
    a disregard for the enemies of linnets and macaws,
fears that match the hawk-haunted buttes out west;

a hard desire for justice, the habit of lip-biting when trouble
    nears, the way my mouth opens like a flower, my quiver
of arrows that outweighs the world, leaving the animals

to bear witness; memories of laughter that was bread and water,
    stylish hats, ways to time-travel, the consequences
of mistakes and second thoughts gummed to the future;

a collection of radios, stacks of vinyl, the limitations
    of secrets, long nights that cascade like waterfalls,
my madness, granular and complex, sealed like a footfall.

A BRIEF REFLECTION ON TORTURE
NEAR THE LIBRARY OF CONGRESS

Shouldering a bag of great literature, you glimpse spider silk
extruding from spinnerets, spiraling into
an orb above a restaurant's *Exit* sign. Revenue questions
aside, a diplomat's diamond shirt-studs
sparkle beside Ritzenhoff Cristal just when you recall
bike-riding as a child behind a laundry truck,
its bouquets of lavender spraying the road.

Innocuous the lightness of transactions,
exchanging hands, cash touching in meetings.
Some memories are made for the hatchet's blade.
But the dissidents are rioting today, and a cable station away
above the bar in slow motion a player tosses chalk
into the air like a spell and suddenly you smell
newly opened wads of fresh paper bills.

Yours is the study of steam or how the mind
sprinklers, presently irrigating. Somewhere,
someone is screaming for holy intervention
in a military prison. Once, below a cathedral

of trees with signs along the road that read
Chutes de branches, you pictured a torture table.
The bag now feels like a century of offenses.

THE CLOISTERED LIFE OF NUNS

In Reading Market, you recall a fisherman in Sifnos
fetch a snapper sloshing in a tub, the quick motions
of snipping needlepoint fins, and, tail to head,
rake with the back side of a fillet knife
so that little translucent scales seem to burst
like a frenzy of designs from the Age of Enlightenment.

The mind sweeps empty opening into night.

A poacher hacks the face of an elephant and
tugs at ivory tusk as the driver listens
to Ragamuffin while reading Job 40:15.

Suppose there is an Architect or a Gnostic,
what consciousness could we ever possess?
What then of the discontents rioting today?
On a spatial scale, Plato held the ideal
Republic should glimmer into sight.

A German shepherd barks at a rabbit secreted in a hedgerow
over genial chatter at a Hamptons summer party
as water striders dog-paddle on a man-made pond in sync.

The carnage as a way of life like a plain gold
ring inscribed with a single word: Darwin.

You touched a peach and saw in your mind
the cloistered life of nuns descending
stairwells like moths. So much crushed ice
spilling out of crates on the floor,
stilled fish eyes marbling.

Behold now behemoth, which I made
with thee; he eateth grass as an ox.

EUROPA

Crossing a darkened sea, Titian's princess
flounces on the back of a muscular moon-white
bull, his coy eyes disguising a god's
predictable lust, the drama of falling drapery
in motion, clutched between her fingers,

and though Titian paints her grasping
the bull's garlanded horn, her tumbling body caught
between disbelief and the sudden knowledge,
a mother's warnings of what will surely come,
that even the once-gentle are disguised
beasts, and what most maidens on
the seashore know, his enchantment
is not of this world, and her acquiescence
will never come, the canvas a frozen
portrait, silence and capitulation.

And yet the great painter empties
one cupid's hand of its quiver, a lone bow inviting
doubt. We gaze on her flesh, Titian's triumph,
that makes of us a sudden tribunal who wonder, how much
her open mouth and rapturous twisting her own.

———

Abruptly the sea at the center of the painting,
now a gulf, torn clouds
blend into craggy mountains.

MY SON AND ME

At the bar in Otto's near Fifth,
both off from work, the heavy
foot traffic of silhouetted commuters
hastening home outside, and us, here
two drinks in. The conversation
has just ramped up and he wants
to know why I did it, how I could have betrayed
our family. The bartender is in night school,

we learn, for law, but, meanwhile, he can name
all the great vineyards in Sonoma,
and how many laborers worked the field
and how many the crush pad
last planting season which incidentally he says
gave us some of the best varietals,
he's told, in years: "But it's all really
just a racket though like anything else in life."

I want to tell my son about the great poems
I've taught today yet careful to avoid
the sad lives of the poets, but he has long been
exhausted of lines I recited to him since a child,

my eyes carrying the exuberance of art, and so
would only agitate and call up his condemnation
of my friends as shams parading their
pain as pomp. Instead, I reach for

his hand across the varnished oak top:
"I was disappearing" to which he shakes
his head. I swirl my glass, looking down avidly,
churning the air so as to deliver oxygen
and open up the wine, wishing to
release its veiled bouquet.

I'VE SAID TOO MUCH

I've said too much. The soil overruns with honey.
Porch lights blaze into the afternoons.
I find it difficult to control my idioms; only ask
which direction the wind blows,
and I will give you a history of my elms and
cottonwoods or my theft of fire. My brain plunders
its orchard of speech. Watch the expressionist stains
at the corners of my mouth, dark as blueberries,
blossom into a symphony. I am too far from the land
of hush to be useful. What is said must be said
so I say it. Inheritor of hieroglyphs and cave drawings,
I keep the engines of hearsay fueled,
an echo of the ancients, especially the Sophists.
Leave me with your griefs and barefoot secrets,
and rest assured, I will secure your memory,
and your name, the tremble of a wave heading
to shore will ricochet back into the deep sea
of my sayings and bewilderments. Provide a backdrop
of cheese and tapenades with a little sauvignon
from the Cederberg Mountains and you can have
a lifetime of constellations as you take in the great stone
korai at the Acropolis of Major, unyielding in slanting light.

THE BODY'S UNCONTESTED
NEED TO DEVOUR: AN EXPLANATION

I am bathing again, burying my face
into the great nations of moss.
I am leaning in, smelling the emerald mountains
and the little inhabitants crossing
over rock-like boulders and tree trunks empired
bit by bit. My nose must come to them
like a probing spaceship causing a mighty eclipse.
They speak in whispers but do not shriek
when gazing into the dim landing bays
of my cavernous thoughts. I am grazing
like a Dionysian. I come not with religion.
I come yearning for first spring and a thirst for spores
pooling like mercenaries in the dark.
The little gods of the forest live here.
I want to ingest their verdant settlements
until they carpet my cavities and convert my raptorial
self into its own ecosystem, off into the green.

THE BODY'S UNCONTESTED
NEED TO DEVOUR

or ravishment, the mind
like a candle
guttering that gives
the halls its sparks,

its shadows, which I, for once,
am not ascribing any significance:
no more fire cathedral
made from my terrors and vain insecurities,
no more engine in my throat,
no more little agitated scrap of blaze
sinking below the horizon
I once called *The Artist's Way*.

*

At the bookstore signing table, a woman hands me
a copy of *Holding Company*. I used to
not look them in the eyes and searched
instead their faces for memories of fire (lips),

the rank smell of ashtrays (fingers), someone
weary of moon light (hair).

I sign this plainchant: *I am lonely and death
freezes me*.

VERMONT ECLOGUE

Damp patches of mountain fog. Late afternoon
country roads clamoring for sleep.
Light snow, patient as an assassin, through
leafless branches mists your car.
African masks with half-closed eyes
on a living room wall seem disoriented.
House lights flash on like strong-scented
signals. Below, two moles cross a paddock in
opposite directions. A transient sculpture
of blue jays vaults toward a cluster
of white pines. Behind the thickening sky,
the peaks are shy as migrants.
Earbuds fastened in, you sing, *don't disturb*
this groove, your voice its own woodland
where a man stands at the edge
of a pond watching crystals dissolve in midair.

WINTER

The boughs have been naked for weeks.
Snowplows scrape the highway clean of its sugar.
People withdraw into their nests and study
the language of fire. A group of high school girls
on their way home in the afternoon dark
falls into an embankment and flaps their arms
and legs as though cloud-swimming toward the coming world.
The blank silence of dead earth forces us
to gaze up, harvest the black music that belongs
to all the eyes in the future who will turn to the spheres
and study too whatever light to fill their emptiness.

DEAR ZAKI

—for Ntozake Shange (1948–2018)

like a stream of wet gold floats by my face his words are like that

Thoughts today
of you emerged as I walked
the streets, somewhat frayed
& distraught by more hearsay
of another poet's passing—

this time Gregg
with whom I once shared a beer
after a gig in the Village.
Shamelessly I pelted her
I recall about Gilbert, Grecian

islands, landscapes
that crack both pen & heart.
Despite my bantering & poor taste,
Linda indulged the young upstart
hungry for gossip, our parade

of mistakes. Yet,
what she gave were lessons
on being true to the calling, none
of the angers some
shape into being undone,

but a gratitude
for mornings of coffee
brewed in a briki pot, views
of the Aegean, waves of blue.
his shrill eyes. Glued

to her voice,
I ran a finger along the scarred
oak table, carvings of a couple rejoic
-ing in the fresh chords
of a new love wishing to foist

their joys on
(the lonely? the fallen?)
unsuspecting tenants
in that dark bar: *Dylan*
+ *Diane Forever* within

cupid's arrow.
Her mascara was thick
as a Kollwitz, a heavy sorrow
rivering beneath drift
-ing memories of her Romeo.

The world's full
of absurd men, free
of guilt whose kisses are lures
that hook a would-be bride then flee
leaving musky trails, vapor

-ous hopes, ruined
bodies, the marked scents of beasts,
closed eyes singing bloodlines,
their love of mirrors & creaky
beds. *Her* news reminded

I'd yet named
my debt to you. Once,
David Murray, in concert, claimed
the Painted Bride stage, his famed
Afro-horn found the pulse

———

of the crowd
&, like *Probe*, blew extensions,
to which, behind shades, in bangles, loud,
leopard print, ignoring the too-proud,
you swayed like a palm tree. When

The Love Space
Demands staged the next weeks
I sought local places
you ate, restaurants & boutiques.
I sought your plays, your books,

your nappy
edges, hipster spirit, boho
freedom, you who spoke the holy
order of black poems, so
in the vernacular of us, the tempo

of good-foot
rhythms & wadings in secret
creeks. I felt baptized when you put
in my hands Blakey's Quartet
A Jazz Message at the record

store on Third
out of the blue. Of course
you lived *The Chocolate Works*,
you who would talk Karl Marx,
mamboed from Flatbush to the Bronx.

And all we,
bippies, divas, & black bohos
discussed was you: Zaki
at gallery openings; Zaki
in clubs striking poses.

When you died,
dusk inside eyes everywhere
like Bastille lost Baudelaire,
& the women who feared
rainbows fading from skies,

rubbed out by
the erasers of gray clouds,
lost their dance. Yet, my profound
paradox: I, too, caused enough cry
-ing women to fill a sky.

———————

A young man,
my ambivalence was wide.
I claimed as many as my hands
could hold. Teary-eyed,
their love slammed

into my need
to be loved endlessly
like Christmas all the time. A greed
born of the ego? or a reckless
allegiance to the now? I received

all manner
of guidance from brilliant
women like you, but my pattern
of love-them-then-leave-them
ignored hearts. What use then

this thunder
in the mountains? I've learned
to translate silence, to live under
my own body, the unending alarm
of so much suffering.

———

You knew far
more about the wounds
of men no north star
could heal. We're bound to earth
and wear each other's scars.

IN MEMORY OF
DEREK ALTON WALCOTT

I.

Island traffic slows to a halt
as screeching gulls reluctant
to lift heavenward
congregate like mourners in salt-
crusted kelp as the repellent
news spreads to colder shores:

Sir Derek is no more.
Bandwidths, clogged by streaming
tributes, carry the pitch
of his voice, less so his lines, moored
as they are to a fisherman's who strains
in the Atlantic

then hearing too drops his rod, the reel
unspooling like memory till
his gaped mouth matches
the same look in his wicker creel,

that frozen shock, eyes marble
a different catch.

Pomme-arac trees, sea grapes,
and laurels sway, wrecked having lost
one who heard their leaves'
rustic dialect as law, grasped
their bows as edicts from the first
garden that sowed faith,—

and believe he did, astonished
at the bounty of light, like Adam,
over Castries, Cas-
en-Bas, Port of Spain, the solace
of sonorous rains, clouds like hymns
then edens of grass,

ornate winds on high verandas
carrying spirits who survived
that vile sea-crossing,
who floated up in his stanzas,
the same souls Achille saw alive,
the ocean their coffin,—

faith, too, in sunsets, horizons
whose backlit job is to divide

and spawn reflection
which was his pen's work, reason
twinned with delight, divining
like a church sexton.

Poetry is empty without
discipline, without piety,
he cautions somewhere,
even his lesser rhymes amount
to more than wrought praise but amplify
his poems as high prayer.

So as to earn their wings above,
pelicans move into tactical
formation, then fly
low like jet fighters in honor of
him, nature's mouth, their aerial
salute and goodbye.

II.

Derek, each journey we make
whether Homeric or not
follows the literal wake
of some other craft's launch,

meaning to sense the slightest
motions in unmoving waters
is half the apprentice's
training before he oars

out, careful to coast, break
-ing English's calm surface.
What you admired in Eakins
in conversation at some café

(New Orleans? Philly?) was
how his rower seemed to listen
to ripples on the Schuylkill as
much as to his breath, both silent

on his speaking canvas.
Gratitude made you intolerant
of the rudeness of the avant-
garde or any pronouncements

of the "new," for breathing is
legacy and one's rhythm,
though the blood's authentic
transcription, hems us

to ancestors like a pulse. This,
I fathom, is what you meant
when exalting the merits
of a fellow poet: That man

is at the center of language,
at the center of the song.
Yet a reader belongs to another age
and, likely to list our wrongs

more than the strict triumphs
of our verse, often retreats
like a vanished surf, spume
frothing on a barren beach.

The allure of an artist's works
these days is measured
by his ethics, thus our books,
scrubbed clean, rarely mention

the shadowless dark that settles
over a page like an empire's. Your nib,
like the eye of a moon, flashed into sight
the source of Adam's barbaric cry.

III.

Departed from paradise,
each Nobody a sacrifice,
debating whose lives matter
whereon a golden platter

our eyes roll confused in hate
from Ferguson to Kuwait.
You, maître, gave in laughter
but also for the hereafter

an almost unbearable
truth: we are the terrible
history of warring births
destined for darkest earth.

So as fiber optic lights
bounce under oceans our white
pain, codified as they are
and fiber-layered in Kevlar,

we hear ourselves in you,
where time exiles us to
stand lost as a single nation
awaiting your revelations.

―――――

A shirtless boy, brown as bark,
gallops along shore, bareback
and free on a horse until he fades,
a shimmering, all that remains.

THE ROMANTICS OF
FRANCONIA NOTCH

Matthew Dickman and I are fond
of resurrecting the spotted faces
of state troopers and small-town police
we've met over the years.
We love their melodrama, the way they peel
their aviators in the rearview
of my Jetta as they approach
the car like shy teenagers on a first date
then doff their stiff-brim hats with yellow braids.

There was the pastel-loving cop in Eugene
fond of art deco motels in South Beach,
and the comic book fan in Littleton,
New Hampshire who unlatched his gun
holster, and the one tormented by Goethe's
propositions and thus, led us, choral-like,
through a few hymns before issuing a roadside
warning in Randolph, Vermont.

When they ask us where are we going,
we almost always respond to the town square

of course to give the park back to the wretched
men and their brown bags of sorrow and needles
which turn them to black puddles. We want the crime squad
to know we have a purpose, that we sugar our hopes
with the honeyed lines of Brodsky, Pessoa, and Thoreau
whom we were declaiming just that moment,
zipping in the dark, past low-lit Colonials
when a black bear jumped out as though chased
by the ghost of the bear he used to be and Matthew
turned up Jay-Z's *Black Album* so he'd get
a boost and lurch into further darkness.

URBAN RENEWAL

To work and create "for nothing," . . . to know
that one's creation has no future . . . this is the
difficult wisdom that absurd thought sanctions.
Performing these two tasks simultaneously,
negating on the one hand and magnifying on the
other, is the way open to the absurd creator. He
must give the void its colors.

—*The Myth of Sisyphus*, Albert Camus

WASHINGTON SQUARE

When all that cautions the eyes toward the imminent
slide of autumn to arctic winds, the canopy of English elm
and sycamore leaves like colored coins fall and widen
a hole letting more light spill in, heaven's alms
to earth whose ashen gray and white will soon be all the rage,
our guilty secret is the baby grand playing Glass's *Orphée*
Suite for Piano. Nearby Butoh dancers writhe & almost upstage
with white-painted faces of horror (portraits of Nagasaki?),
and past the fountain's water plumes, a drug-riddled couple
shares the smoldering remains of an American Spirit,
their grizzled dog roped to a shopping cart and frayed duffel
bag, this city's updated version of *American Gothic*.
Our reddish-haired pianist lets the melancholic notes
float to high-rises on Fifth above its triumphal arch,
like a film in reverse where the golden foliage is read by a poet
as autumn's light pours in. "Don't Get Around Much
Anymore," The Ink Spots' Decca cover spins on a phonograph,
an era spiraling soft then held by his gentle pen.

THINKING OF FROST

I thought by now my reverence would have waned,
matured to the tempered silence of the bookish or revealed
how blasé I've grown with age, but the unrestrained
joy I feel when a black skein of geese voyages like a dropped
string from God slowly shifting, when the decayed
apples of an orchard amass beneath its trees like Eve's
first party, when driving and the road Vanna-Whites its crops
of corn whose stalks will soon give way to a harvester's blade
and turn the land to a man's unruly face, makes me believe
I will never soothe the pagan in me, nor exhibit the propriety
of the polite. After a few moons, I'm loud this time of year,
unseemly as a chevron of honking. I'm fire in the leaves,
obstreperous as a New England farmer. I see fear
in the eyes of his children who walk home from school
as evening falls like an advancing trickle of bats, the sky
pungent as bounty in chimney smoke. I read the scowl
below the smiles of parents at my son's soccer game, their agitation,
the figure of wind yellow leaves make of quaking aspens.

xxviii

PARIS

The roaring above rooftops rift me out
of a sleep so violent I knocked my head,
jolting to snare drums and brass at the outer
reaches of wakefulness. 7:14. I misread
a digital clock, then sprung open our rented
terrace window behind the Musée d'Orsay
to see tricolor clouds of France's flag scripted
across the sky over the Champs-Élysées.
Right! Bastille Day. All morning, the marching
of many feet to civic tunes of a country's
pride served as backdrop—some sergeant
in rattling armor and gold epaulettes conducted
when she and I kissed, having survived our clash
of weapons and disloyalties. We had no desire
to gawk with the crowds at passing troops, convoys
of tanks, or watch clumps fall behind cavalries of horse riders.
Instead, I gazed down at her trembling eyelash,
for we had in mind our own drills to stage which garnered
a parade of oohs and aahs, keeping its own cease-fire.

x x i x

NORTH PHILADELPHIA

In the solitary, shaded musk of a storefront
church, abandoned save for secret assembly,
save for slivers of light illuminating drifting motes,
and in the occasional blast across ankles of wintry
air beneath front pews where three women, shawled
and rocking, gathered in a circle late afternoons
as though Sundays were a kind of god-crawl,—
there they groaned, repairing from urban fields, tunes
not so much learned yet risen, earth's laments
gardened in throats from black soil, a slow grumbling,
fitful drawn-out grunts grafting onto gospel notes
not recognized but felt, a ring-shout. Poor folk, troubled
by the devil's work through the week: a cheating
husband, a daughter's addiction, one's house
candled from a gambled paycheck, here rich
in spiritual intimacies, the church dark as a hearse.
I'm still in that dimness, several rows behind their wails,
writing their moans coming through like Braille.

FISH & WILDLIFE

The lake's cold shacks of ice-fishing anglers
speed by like homeless shanties. This is North Country,
where a cabin's fireplace wears moose antlers,
where the mesmeric drift of snow snakes Route 30
sending a chalk-white F-150 plummeting into a ditch.
Icicles hover above like liquid spears.
A shawled neighbor in silhouette is a witch
but you believe in the company of man and seek a cold beer
and the crackling fire of a bar up the road whose patrons'
talk of deadly snowmobiles steams its front
window. Gossip turns the evening darker, and the nation
might as well be this small shadowy room half in hunting
gear, eyeing the woman holding a cue at a haloed
pool table. Outside, a grumbling snowplow barrels up
the street like a middle linebacker. A truckload
of modern furniture sits in the parking lot. Yep,
someone says to a Patriots loss: Shoulda won that
one. The almost bare streets seem clutched
in ice, wind dusting up crystals in orange streetlight.
Old men in Franklin County dream of being touched.

DOUBLE VIEW OF THE ADIRONDACKS
AS REFLECTED OVER LAKE CHAMPLAIN
FROM WATERFRONT PARK

The mountains are at their theater again,
each ridge practicing an oration of scale and crest,
and the sails, performing glides across the lake, complain
of being outshadowed despite their gracious
bows. Thirteen years in this state, what hasn't occurred?
A cyclone in my spirit led to divorce, four books
gave darkness an echo of control, my slurred
hand finding steadiness by the prop of a page,
and God, my children whom I scarred! Pray they forgive.
My crimes felt mountainous, yet perspective
came with distance, and like those peaks, once keening
beneath biting ice, then felt resurrection in a vestige
of water, unfrozen, cascading and adding to the lake's
depth, such have I come to gauge my own screaming.
The masts tip so far they appear to capsize, keeling
over where every father is a boat on water. The wakes
carry the memory of battles, and the Adirondacks
hold their measure. I am a tributary of something greater.

THE VALKYRIE

The land nearly erased, the mountains flee.
Another arctic blast of snow falls on the peaks
concealing that panorama which first bewitched
my breath where now across the valley wind gusts kick
up land clouds akin to silvery explosions
trip-wired by some aimless deer whose timid motions
break into a sudden sprint across a logging road
then up a gnarled hillside of saplings and dense trees. Slow
wars within begin this way, a vaporous fog
from which I've sought a path out of the monologue
in my head: I've no true friends, my verse's
mediocre at best, a white captivity of rehearsed
caustic thoughts that mist in layers and blind
reason. Then reversing my iceberg mind,
always her with that voice bright as a cardinal
and campfire hands leading me past glacial
snowpiles. Everywhere icicles collect like daggers;
subzero air cuts through harsh as Wagner's
Die Walküre. We've survived blizzard nights,
both of us refunding earth's stolen daylight.

xxxiii

A GRANDFATHER'S LECTURE

If punched, you punch twice as hard, and in the face,
a wop right in the nose. Use the flat counter of your fist
or the palm's hard ridge. Lean into it but brace
your stroke with your back leg then lift
your whole blow into his mug. He'll crumble.
If you're lucky, blood will pour in rivulets
down his mouth and chin leaving him startled,
dazed like the newly awakened. Don't relent.
Think what he'd do to you if given the chance.
Throw what we used to call a haymaker.
Nest fear inside but don't tremble. Don't parade & prance
like you're Ali. Don't hesitate. Land a jawbreaker,
jab him in the gut. Did you know the Brown Bomber
never televised a hit, never reared back, just snuggled in,
leaned close shoulder to shoulder, calmer
than most then kapow to his ribs? Schmeling struggled
on the ropes. Life's no boxing ring, but know your power,
what your shadow is made. Then always make up.
Show your adversary you've got class; don't tower
over him. That's for punks. Extend a hand. Help him up.

THE ABSURD MAN SUITE

I want to liberate my universe of its phantoms
and to people it solely with flesh-and-blood truths
whose presence I cannot deny.

—Albert Camus

THE ABSURD MAN AT FOURTEEN

After church in an empty parking lot one Sunday
facing the Schuylkill, my mother wept
behind a steering wheel. My feet throbbed
in a pair of Buster Browns I'd outgrown
by a season as I looked out the window,
autumn performing its last dying.

He punched her again, a woman called the house,
some yelling then us out the door leaving
the kitchen phone cord swinging.

Morning light burnished the windshield.
Her wet face made her holy. A lone
sculler scissored the river, his silhouette
a shadow in motion. I wanted to say
something but my eyes flamed wild
as reddish orange leaves firing
up the ground. His stony look as we left
said he was tormentor and master.

———

I let her cry, and felt a new world
of women grow around me,
and when she reached for my hand
instinctively I pulled away, her mouth
open to my fading, unbearable heart.

VISITATION

When his dead mother reappears in a storefront glass
behind him somber as a midweek
wake, he knows it's time to count
his reflections. He worries
when scars heal too fast
or when a memory of flames threads
his body like a cutthroat waltz. His body
hardened into a rainy nightfall, sleepwalking
a vortex of honeysuckle and wild hearts.
Let him glimpse himself too long,
and he will put a lantern brightness to his eyes
hoping to crowd out ghosts reaching
like moths across eternity with broken wings.

3

AUGUSTINIAN

Like a sage walking a dirt road
muddied from an afternoon rain, he feels
less the aristocrat given his threadbare deeds,
his less than noble teeth, the way he squanders
second chances only to excel at a kind of
blind teetering like a mole in a cave.

He accepts rainclouds the way he accepts aspirin.
What is left to be said only that he followed
desire's holy waves Chagall-like across rooftops,
itself a religion, and fastened his embarrassments
to tales of hocus-pocus. Broken whispers
and miles to go. So as not to look pupil-less,

he meditates until his peace lengthens
to a bubble on water, glass consciousness.
The laundered napkin, smooth on his lap, turns
his knee to just another white hill.

4

WHAT HAPPENED

When I closed the back door, the pole-lit
night streets beckoned through pools
of shadows, the sidewalks barren yet hard
with desire. I left my wife entrenched in her prison
of dreams facing her bedside clock ticking
off the minutes and our wedding picture layered
in its film of dust and our blanketed son beneath
a mobile of zoo creatures spinning in a suspended carousel.
I powered down the car window and listened
to night birds' quarreling chirps. Patches of grass grew
heavy with dew and families of watchful deer sauntered
like migrants over garden beds. With each turn
of the steering wheel, our lives disappeared. Hissing
tires took me to a province of flames. A wind hot
as a simoom swept along my skin. A voice approached
out of votive darkness. Next I was walking through
the halls of Dis guided by a hand toward a wild braid of pain.

5

THE DAY AFTER

Light glittering its knives on the waterfront
lake all the way down Main, I walked
through the door of my sorrows, dust visibly
floating tiny as sins only to settle on a walnut sideboard
where sat the photo taken that first summer,
she and I, no longer submerged,
dripping in water having come up for air,
both of us unknowing then of the edges
of our appetites, our embankments of silence,
the soon desolation of our bodies.

I lay down bewildered on the living room floor.
The curtains still, the rooms
tormented by my voice.

6

EUROPA REVISITED

Even though we commune as adults,
consenting, one or more arrives
with orb and scepter, measures
of rule like ordering birds to fly into wind.

To bend to the glance of another, the tender
surrender, stillness in the royal eyes
to honor the softest part of the self,
reverence equal to our own, invites

the will of intimacy. For cathedrals,
for Gothic spires and vaulted ceilings, conjure
scenes of submission to deities as smoke rises
and scatters its tendrils to the last winds of philosophy.

I fear, I fear the monument
we make with tongue and immaculate thoughts,
merely an assembly for our noiseless and insatiable bodies.

7

THE MOST BEAUTIFUL MAN NEVER
PERFORMS HARD LABOR

I am sure my grandfather would be ashamed
of my hands for they carry nothing and are soft
as downy feathers, and I am sure he'd look
askance at my treasured collection of stemless wineglasses

and fashionable ascots; I am sure he'd smirk at the sight
of fresh cut flowers delivered at my door Tuesday afternoons
when my silken thoughts make like schools of minnows,
and so, too, the cantatas filling my house, and me, paddling

like a dog through the recitatives, so unaccustomed
my hands to the shape and feel of a revolver or the wood
shaving tools he kept in his tool belt like armaments;
I am sure he'd shake his head at my having paused beneath

a fruit tree on a bicycle with a basket, carrying a French baguette
& a collection of Lorca's poetry, angling for a woman's touch.

THE ABSURD MAN ON OBJET PETIT A'

In movies, the bad guy stands-off face
to face with the good guy. They are wanted
in each other's town, but we know
as moviegoers they are the same person
and could win a look-alike contest
if one were more famous than the other.

Our recognition of form and content,
or Lacan's mirror stage, takes us
above the clouds in the late style
of midcentury Dutch chairs
and talk analysis.

The two would do well to lick the other's birthmarks
except for desire is two pistols observed
in an optical field, *mise en abyme*, forming a kind
of blissed-out symmetry,
or so thinks Major.

In a 1970's advertisement, a woman lays
on the glassy hood of a Fiat Spider;
this, too, requires us to stand oblique
to our own image. Ponder, for example,
Holbein's *The Ambassadors*.
Nobody wins.

THE ABSURD MAN HAS PINK-EYE

Winter rush-hour traffic gets us through our living—
way stations and errors—what in the end
amounts to the appeal of parking lights
blistering bumper-to-bumper like one red church
pulsating the road's skin, but the strain
of modern existence overruns the banks
of our eyelids especially when wolfish strategies
reveal themselves to us more than to our neighbors
who right now, as we speak, are skinning a bear
in North Country, plaid shirts ballooning.

In short, driving on slushy roads in late-afternoon dark,
that arsenal of irritating news about red states
and blue states on public radio hurts,
even if delivered philosophically like champagne
bubbles obliterated once they reach the top.

PLAY MONEY

Like whatever fires that chose us,
I kept coming back to that foamy wake
of water where she kicked
and, not so much distracted as suddenly
pledged to observe, heard
where once were beaten waves,
tranquil breathing,
my own.

Isn't this the nature of repose
when one's life is a matinee
for all the professors starved
for divinity? Sometimes we stand

together in checkout lines
in feverish objectivity—
the puzzle of bagging a life
so that unbagging does more than reverse
like Orpheus, but cast us forward
to some future communion.

————————

When the cashier asks, "How will
we be paying," I pull out of my
front pocket, poems and more poems.

ORACLE & PROPHECY

What I learned to endure was not the weight
of an evaporated wallet or squirrelly women improvising
mincing steps across city streets but simply
the mechanical dance of living, and having since learned
the precise count of ballroom steps toward my children, these days,
I stay indoors and watch carpet fibers grow around
my planted feet or dust bunnies gather like a conference
of aspiring clouds outside my bedroom door. This was life
in the vale: amatory flicks conjured in whispered
late-night disclosures scene after inglorious scene.
Picture a spotlight onstage, alone, staring at a low-domed oculus
when sure as stars I was the pedestal and the monument,
the oracle and the prophecy touched by a void.
Yes, one could make a documentary of my running man
or my blues trot, but I'd rather you meet me in the next sentence:
This body is no longer a passing prayer sung by those fearful of time.

THE ABSURD MAN DISPENSES ADVICE

If your mouth is stucco and your crush
is lakefront, what manner of ivy
should wrist your serve? Try avoiding
the verve of leather interiors
with boys whose menacing faces and over-
the-shoulder sweaters augur begrudging
expressions of fall-catalogue bliss.

Don't grow thin, enjoy exhalations
of cold breaths after ice-cream breaks.

You are more earth than potted plants
in a sunroom, and besides, someday the Shakers
will return to the playground able-voiced,
carrying long-ladders, deep in song.

HOW TO AVOID A CRASH

Some mornings riding to work
on a road bike up a busy thoroughfare,
my hands tight around the handlebars,
I think of my secrets, a slaughterhouse of whispers.

Near the off-ramp, a semitruck's tires squeal
hard up ahead and exhaust fumes nearly blind
as I navigate periodic surges and tons of metal
accelerating by like oversized munitions.

They held tight, like me, full of an emptiness
we so longed to supplant with desire, our muscles
rough pedaling toward an imaginary terminus.

Now I make eye contact, as experts suggest,
with others whose loud music from open windows
or makeup appliqués have no chance
of sending them swerving in my direction,
jarring me off a path I work to keep,
catapulting me, eyes full of terror, over a median
and down the road's unforgiving blacktop.

DR. BOVARY TO MONSIEUR DUPUIS
(ALT. TAKE 1)

What leads me to email you, grief and anger.
I know what transpired in the cab you made a bed.
I'll not quit until the world knows the philanderer
you are, until I've put a bullet in your head.

OUR EYES WERE FAR AWAY

Our eyes were far away, as were
the hills writing their own memoirs,
marking our stark absence,
our blue-faced emptiness.

We believed what we felt then
till our doctrines signaled
nothing. Naked, we woke
to our islands and dressed

having canceled the tour.
In the corner, there was a mirror
but the prophets were there
sequestered, withdrawn.

Our sculptures revealed
remote testimonies. Who revolted
as fresh hatreds swept
across our faces while we slept?

———

We walked past the coffin
of what we once were, the dead
awakened, no longer safe
in our siestas. We thought we said

everything. We hadn't.
Bloodstained, we now raise
a bandaged hand and pen. Where
we want to go has no name.

WHY THE ABSURD MAN DOESN'T
DANCE ANYMORE

Singular the pressure our eyes nights
when the body hungers for the music
    of the bones only religion, flashing here

and there like those of a carnivorous bird,
its hard beak, where women and men come
    out evenings for supper, and this world

is rendered in swirling white lights and
diamonds on a dance floor, where a mixmaster's
    swelter of programmable handclaps

or deep bass kicks leads to accidental
body brushes, arabesques, the hallucination
    of grinding moves, a kind of leave-taking then,

a look over the shoulder before squaring off
to wiggle into the latest craze which has
    always been allegorical for the assorted

playhouses of the flesh, how fingers and voice stream
to work on (let's admit) a stranger's spirit
    in a city on the brink of a nervous collapse,

the mouth a pulpit of post-breathing, wet
the neck's straining muscles, its own arousal
    machine, where the need burns in sync

with a woman's twirling red dress, pinched
between forefingers and thumbs and hiked
    to reveal thighs lonesome as horses in a field,

where shuffling footsteps suddenly glide like
gunships across a sea, taking a chance on the past
    & the questions humming inside our heads.

THE ABSURD MAN SWIPES
LEFT IN NEW YORK

What accounting we performed on
our feelings made all those convincing
expressions of *amore* more like scattered
spent balloons when the party has died down
to a post-election speech and the loser shushes
an injured crowd, offering jump-rope support for his opponent.

Please drop the needle again. As so often happens,
we are without a cement foundation or a caisson,
and one of us is sitting by a red rotary phone
playing "Time is on my side! Yes it is!"
I hate courtships like I hate circulars;
all that false advertisement just to get me in the door.

Vintage phonographs are back in, and so too
Sunday morning staticky intros with Bloody Marys.
Some are tuberous dahlias doing a number
in our gardens. They can only say something
annually, unlike tubas which though dormant

in cases by humming refrigerators in cramped prewars
in Manhattan, shine brassily to some silent
march, some victory ahead.

That's what we get for checking our debits and credits,
a lukewarm ecosystem in our heads,
plenty of doubts when we all know
the world is one feverish jungle.
And our profit and loss reports?
A single seething statement of our turpitude.

NO ONE FORGETS

Today I am describing evil near Sugar Hill
and Franconia Notch, recalling my sixth
grade teacher again and the classroom
that launched my meadow of brooding
and how I was given a café of songs
farmed and fertilized in the palm of my hands
by wooden rulers taped together in another century.
Each of us will encounter a woman
from those years when we awkwardly looked
in the mirror and tried the latest dance craze
or stared down at our midriff and considered
its potential for satisfying some deity
with fresh oracles of underarm hair.
The body lives a life that is not ours.
Some evening, quite soon, my son will return home
and say "I give up," his eyes exhausted from all the bar lights,
his fingers stained & brittle as moth-wings,
the wet kisses of his life already fading from his spongy lips.
We will compare our sorrows and the roadkill
we drove over as the car windows
darkened in a valley of somber mountains.

THE ABSURD MAN IN THE MIRROR
for Didi

At sunset, winter mountains reach
across a page the color of honey.
Sometimes my hands want
all of her syllables.
I walk in kindness
when she's around
which is to say I feel
Chaplinesque. I mend myself
because she hungers
for golden peaks.
The eastern horizon
offers its diamonds
which we stash
in silent mumblings.
When she speaks, I feel
unburied yet hear still the dead
of my own house. No one cares
that I count her eye blinks.
No one cares about all this hard water.
The hours are tall as polar caps.

NOW THAT YOU ARE HERE, I CAN THINK

What you really are is svelte,
the mainland of your feelings
a young Veronica Webb, and what we share
are solutions, and not so much
the Parisian air you tired of, nor the fat,
sweaty bead coursing a décolletage,
an unlikely consequence of the Kyoto
Protocol, but the pleasures
of lounging below French-style
windows open wide as arms whose blowsy
curtain is a shawl that formally hangs
and informally shifts when you
drift into the room like
a Spike Lee dolly shot.

The kids are dancing to some Ariana,
but I'm watching what you do
with your lips when reading silently
around 4:22 p.m. on a late Sunday afternoon.

I have a weakness for marble winding
stairs and tight two-person elevators.
But the brasseries are waiting
as well as the *fútbol* fans who need help
cheering, for we are Americans after all
and are ready to hype even the locusts on the day
of judgment. I don't care about the midfielder
or the winger. You're smiling, and that's all
the defending I'll ever need.

THE ABSURD MAN FREED OF
HIS INNOCENCE

All evening,
I've listened to my mind
revving in the garage
of my unwakened life, the driver's seat
empty save for crumbs
lodged in leather creases.

A muffled music surges
periodically up through
the floorboards
between bouts of static
which carries the soft, faded
voice of my mother
saying she wants
to be remembered.

The door has no handle
to lift, and the animals
of my freedom lie trapped.
Where I want to go
has no name.

PAPER DOLLS AT THE MET

I'm suffering again that feeling
of being robbed; everyone's socially
blossoming at The Gala.
My coffee is cold and people
are using my looks.

I, too, would like to move
like an African cat
maybe a caracal
one big slow dance
a hundred clicking flashes
per second.

Each year the glamourous
grow less glamourous
and I'm out of town
refusing to bloom
all Winnie-the-Pooh-like.

My third eye blinks
in my hand: self-
immolating kimonos
sift away. I don't get
the avant-garde.

Something about all this masking
and invisible human thunder
roaring in a sequin.

Keep your good weather to
yourself I tell The New Impressionists.
Your entrance is all wrong.

THE ABSURD MAN IS SUBJECT
TO PAREIDOLIA

No one believes in angels.
The hills appear lost.
The president waves routinely.
At dusk, the passing towns gather all
their charms and give them to the coming night,
the body's coffin.

The dashboard's panel is a commercial
break from the mind of forest,
music burning in the seeds.

"If not for angels, we'd fall to more wars,"
I say, "and my love weighs
more than the universe.
Don't ask me to explain this."
Car beams fall on the trees.

Something shows between
the branches, taking shape.
I know I'll suffer this plague forever.

NOTHING TO SEE HERE, MOVE ALONG

All through my days, elaborate silken rays
coming through screens carrying
its own occult. I am in the habit of questioning love
which is a storm of rare light
silvering spider webs in a sacred forest,
the silent clock in the town square,
the heavy footprints of the homeless,
the museum we do not enter.

So when I say I've subdued
the stallions raging in my blood,
know that I travel here only to watch
the sparrow hawk flying low over marl prairie,
to take in the sedge wren's flits and jukes
like teenagers learning a new dance.
I'm here guarding my freedom,
rubbing my hands over yesterday fires.

DOUBLE MAJOR

I emerge whenever he confuses the lamp for a moon.

It is then he thinks of fine bindings in ordered athenaeums.

I own his face, but he washes and spends too little time behind his ears.

He sees me in the mirror behind thick clouds of shaving
    cream then suddenly believes in ghosts.

His other selves are murals in the cave of his mind. They are speechless
    yet large. They steer his wishes like summer rain and amplify
    his terrors like newscasters.

What he doesn't know: his dreams are his father's dreams, which are his
    grandfather's dreams, and so on. *They* possessed a single wish.

He knocks repeatedly on the bolted door to his imagination.

Tragically, he believes he can mend his wounds with his poetry.

And thus, I am his most loyal critic. He trots me out like a police dog.

He calls our thirst for pads and pencils destiny.

Our voices come together like two wings of a butterfly.

On occasion, he closes his eyes and sees me.

I am negative capability: the test to *all men are created equal.*

We are likely to dance at weddings against my will. He pulled out the same
    moves writing this poem, a smooth shimmy and a hop.

This page is a kind of looking glass making strange whatever stone carvings
　　he installed along the narrow road to his interior.
I suffer in silence wedded to his convictions. He would like to tell you
　　the truth about love. But we are going to bed, to bed.

ACKNOWLEDGMENTS

Grateful acknowledgement is made to the editors of the following publications in which some of these poems appeared, often in slightly altered form: the Academy of American Poets' *Poem-a-Day*, *The American Scholar*, *Art in Print*, *Boston Review*, *Callaloo*, *Hunger Mountain*, *Iowa Review*, *Literary Imagination*, *The Paris Review*, *Ploughshares*, *Post Road*, *The Southampton Review*, *The Virginia Quarterly Review*, and *World Literature Today*.

This book features poems in collaboration with artist Jane Kent ("The Flâneur Tends a Well-Liked Summer Cocktail" featured in *Art in Print*) and Jill Moser ("Urban Renewal" featured in *The Southampton Review*). I wish to thank them for their friendship and patience, even more for lending their brilliance and creativity to illuminating beyond the limits of language.

Kerrin McCadden and Elizabeth A. Powell generously provided invaluable feedback on drafts of these poems. To them, and other members of The Vermont School, I offer heartfelt gratitude. I wish to also thank David Lehman, Stacey Harwood-Lehman, and Mark Bibbins for the pleasures and gift of reading American poetry while also writing this book. And to Didi Jackson: some wounds do heal. Thank you for your nourishing love, care, tolerance, and fastidiousness, even more for bringing your poetry into my world.